Agatha Christie ®

WRITER'S
JOURNAL

CHRONICLE BOOKS
SAN FRANCISCO

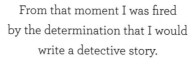

From that moment I was fired
by the determination that I would
write a detective story.

—Agatha Christie, *An Autobiography* (1975)

THIS JOURNAL BELONGS TO:

An author's business is simply to write. Writers are diffident creatures—they need encouragement.

—Agatha Christie, *An Autobiography* (1975)

The creative urge can come out in any
form: in embroidery, in the cooking of
interesting dishes, in painting, drawing
and sculpture, in composing music,
as well as in writing books and stories.

—Agatha Christie, *An Autobiography* (1975)

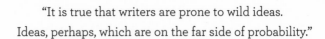

"It is true that writers are prone to wild ideas.
Ideas, perhaps, which are on the far side of probability."

—Poirot, *Hallowe'en Party* (1969)

"I'm too busy writing or rather worrying because I can't write. That's really the most tiresome thing about writing— though everything is tiresome really, except the one moment when you get what you think is going to be a wonderful idea, and can hardly wait to begin."

—Ariadne Oliver, *The Pale Horse* (1961)

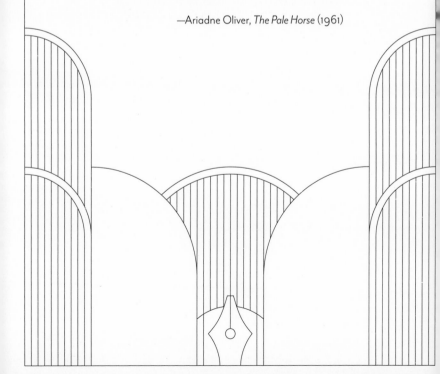

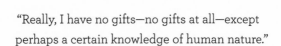

"Really, I have no gifts—no gifts at all—except perhaps a certain knowledge of human nature."

—Miss Marple, *A Murder is Announced* (1950)

Of course, all the practical details are still
to be worked out, and the people have
to creep slowly into my consciousness,
but I jot down my splendid idea in an
exercise book.

—Agatha Christie, *An Autobiography* (1975)

"Method and order, they are everything."

—Poirot, *Death on the Nile* (1937)

_____

_____

_____

_____

_____

_____

_____

_____

_____

_____

_____

_____

_____

_____

_____

_____

_____

_____

It is a pleasure sometimes, when looking
vaguely through a pile of old note-books,
to find something scribbled down, as:
*Possible plot—do it yourself—Girl and
not really sister—August*—with a kind of
sketch of a plot. What it's all about I can't
remember now; but it often stimulates me,
if not to write that identical plot, at least
to write something else.

—Agatha Christie, *An Autobiography* (1975)

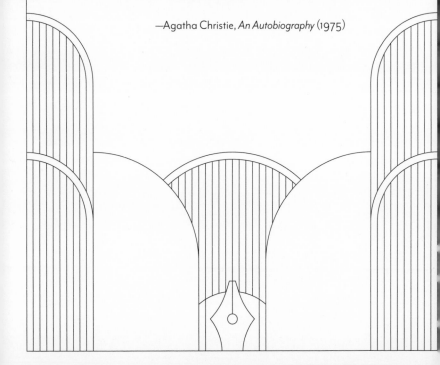

"Human nature is much the same in a village as anywhere else, only one has opportunities and leisure for seeing it at closer quarters."

—Miss Marple, "The Companion" (1930)

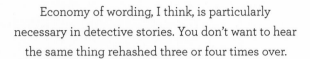

Economy of wording, I think, is particularly necessary in detective stories. You don't want to hear the same thing rehashed three or four times over.

—Agatha Christie, *An Autobiography* (1975)

I was, I suppose, always over-burdened
with imagination. That has served me well
in my profession—it must, indeed, be the
basis of the novelist's craft . . .

—Agatha Christie, *An Autobiography* (1975)

"*If* one is going to tell a lie at all, it might
as well be an artistic lie, a romantic lie,
a convincing lie!"

—Poirot, *Dumb Witness* (1937)

I never had a definite place which was *my* room or where I retired specially to write. . . . All I needed was a steady table and a typewriter.

—Agatha Christie, *An Autobiography* (1975)

"It has seemed to me from the beginning that either this crime was very simple— so simple that it was difficult to believe its simplicity (and simplicity, Mademoiselle, can be strangely baffling) or else it was extremely complex."

—Poirot, *The Hollow* (1946)

"I've often noticed that once coincidences
start happening they go on happening
in the most extraordinary way. I dare
say it's some natural law that we haven't
found out."

—Tuppence Beresford, *The Secret Adversary* (1922)

The really safe and satisfactory place to work out a story in your mind is when you are washing up. The purely mechanical labour helps the flow of ideas and how delightful to find your domestic task finished with no actual remembrance of having done it! I strongly recommend domestic routine for all those engaged in creative thinking.

—Agatha Christie,
Foreword to *The Labours of Hercules* (1947)

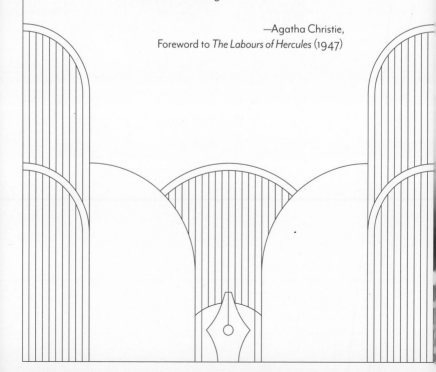

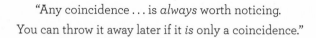

"Any coincidence . . . is *always* worth noticing.
You can throw it away later if it *is* only a coincidence."

—Miss Marple, *Nemesis* (1971)

_____

_____

_____

_____

_____

_____

_____

_____

_____

_____

_____

_____

_____

_____

_____

_____

_____

It had been exciting, to begin with, to be writing books—partly because, as I did not feel I was a real author, it was each time astonishing that I should be able to write books that were actually *published*.

—Agatha Christie, *An Autobiography* (1975)

"One actually has to *think*, you know. And thinking is always a bore. And you have to plan things. And then one gets stuck every now and then, and you feel you'll never get out of the mess—but you do!"

—Ariadne Oliver, *Cards on the Table* (1936)

I could live in the book amongst the people I was writing about, and mutter their conversations and see them striding about the room I had invented for them.

—Agatha Christie, *An Autobiography* (1975)

"There you are, Ariadne. . . . The whole plot of your next novel presented to you. All you'll have to do is work in a few false clues, and—of course—do the actual writing."

—Robin Upward, *Mrs McGinty's Dead* (1952)

The two essentials for a story were a title
and a plot ... sometimes the title led to
a plot all by itself, as it were, and then all
was plain sailing.

—"The Witness for the Prosecution" (1925)

"The personality of a criminal, Georges, is
an interesting matter. Many murderers are
men of great personal charm."

—Poirot, *The Mystery of the Blue Train* (1928)

I felt slightly embarrassed if I was going to write. Once I could get away, however, shut the door and get people not to interrupt me, then I was able to go full speed ahead, completely lost in what I was doing.

—Agatha Christie, *An Autobiography* (1975)

"Writing's not particularly enjoyable.
It's hard work like everything else."

—Ariadne Oliver, *Cards on the Table* (1936)

A sudden excitement would come over
me and I would rush off to write down
what I felt gurgling round in my mind.

—Agatha Christie, *An Autobiography* (1975)

"Motives for murder are sometimes very trivial, Madame. . . . Most frequent— money. . . . Then there is revenge, and love, and fear—and pure hate, and beneficence—"

—Poirot, *Death on the Nile* (1937)

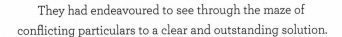

They had endeavoured to see through the maze of conflicting particulars to a clear and outstanding solution.

—Murder on the Orient Express (1934)

_____

_____

_____

_____

_____

_____

_____

_____

_____

_____

_____

_____

_____

_____

_____

_____

_____

_____

_____

I was so frightened of interruptions, of anything breaking the flow of continuity, that after I had written the first chapter in a white heat, I proceeded to write the last chapter, because I knew so clearly where I was going that I felt I must get it down on paper.

—Agatha Christie, *An Autobiography* (1975)

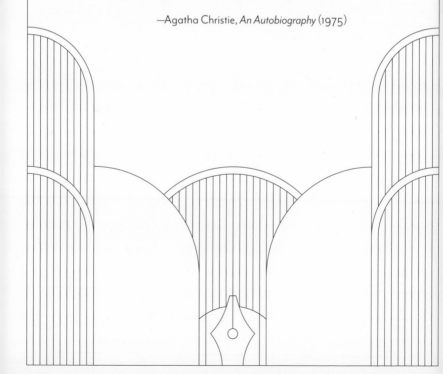

"Murderers always find it difficult to keep things simple. They can't keep themselves from elaborating."

—Miss Marple, *A Caribbean Mystery* (1964)

I assumed the burden of a profession,
which is to write even when you don't want
to, don't much like what you are writing,
and aren't writing particularly well.

—Agatha Christie, *An Autobiography* (1975)

It's no good starting out by thinking one
is a heaven-born genius—some people are,
but very few. No, one is a tradesman—
a tradesman in a good honest trade. You
must learn the technical skills, and then,
within that trade, you can apply your own
creative ideas; but you must submit to
the discipline of form.

—Agatha Christie, *An Autobiography* (1975)

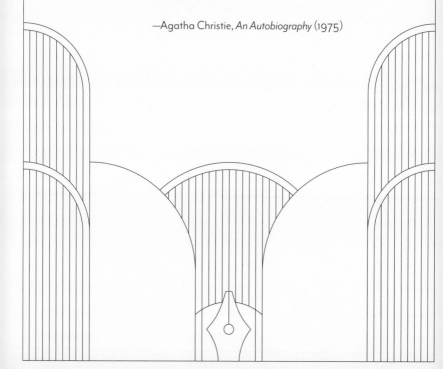

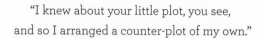

"I knew about your little plot, you see,
and so I arranged a counter-plot of my own."

—Poirot, "The Adventure of the Christmas Pudding" (1960)

There is always, of course, that terrible
three weeks, or a month, which you have
to get through when you are trying to
get started on a book. There is no agony
like it. You sit in a room, biting pencils,
looking at a typewriter, walking about,
or casting yourself down on a sofa, feeling
you want to cry your head off. . . . And
yet it seems that this particular phase
of misery has got to be lived through.

—Agatha Christie, *An Autobiography* (1975)

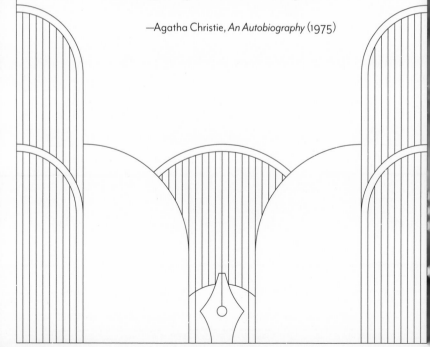

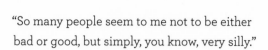

"So many people seem to me not to be either
bad or good, but simply, you know, very silly."

—Miss Marple, "The Tuesday Night Club" (1927)

"In moments of great stress, the mind focuses itself upon some quite unimportant matter which is remembered long afterwards with the utmost fidelity, driven in, as it were, by the mental stress of the moment. It may be some quite irrelevant detail, like the pattern of a wallpaper, but it will never be forgotten."

—Mr Quin, "The Coming of Mr Quin" (1924)

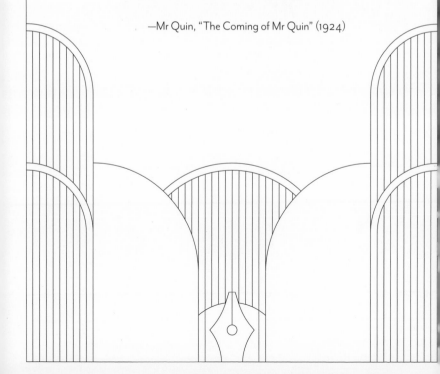

Sometimes I think that is the moment
one feels nearest to God, because you
have been allowed to feel a little of the
joy of pure creation. You have been able
to make something that is not yourself.

—Agatha Christie, *An Autobiography* (1975)

People are capable of surprising one frightfully. One gets an idea of them into one's head, and sometimes it's absolutely wrong.

—*Crooked House* (1949)

One of the pleasures of writing detective stories is that there are so many types to choose from: the light-hearted thriller, which is particularly pleasant to do; the intricate detective story with an involved plot which is technically interesting and requires a great deal of work, but is always rewarding; and then what I can only describe as the detective story that has a kind of passion behind it—that passion being to help save innocence. Because it is *innocence* that matters, not *guilt*.

—Agatha Christie, *An Autobiography* (1975)

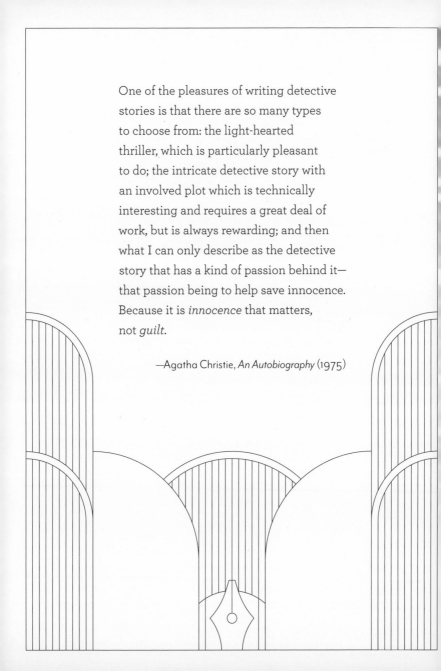

"I wanted to sit quietly and write my book."

—Edmund Swettenham, *A Murder is Announced* (1950)

Like all young writers, I was trying to
put far too much plot into one book.

—Agatha Christie, *An Autobiography* (1975)

"One does not, you know, employ merely the muscles. I do not need to bend and measure the footprints and pick up the cigarette ends and examine the bent blades of grass. It is enough for me to sit back in my chair and *think*."

—Poirot, *Five Little Pigs* (1942)

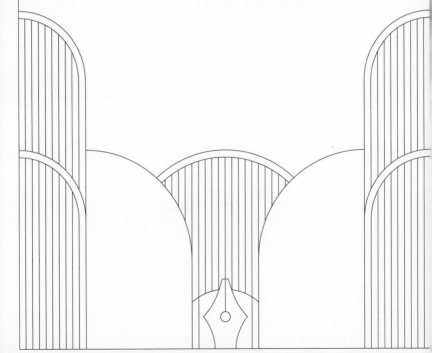

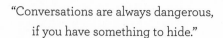

"Conversations are always dangerous,
if you have something to hide."

—Miss Marple, *A Caribbean Mystery* (1964)

_____

_____

_____

_____

_____

_____

_____

_____

_____

_____

_____

_____

_____

_____

_____

_____

_____

"It's never difficult to *think* of things. . . .
The trouble is that you think of too many,
and then it all becomes too complicated,
so you have to relinquish some of them
and that *is* rather agony."

—Ariadne Oliver, *Dead Man's Folly* (1956)

"There are no short cuts."

—Mr Justice Wargrave,
And Then There Were None (1939)

Plots come to me at such odd moments: when I am walking along a street, or examining a hat-shop with particular interest, suddenly a splendid idea comes into my head, and I think, "Now that would be a neat way of covering up the crime so that nobody would see the point."

—Agatha Christie, *An Autobiography* (1975)

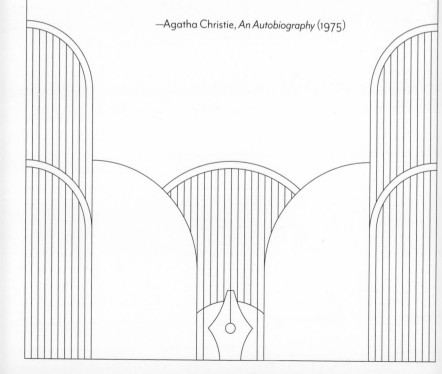

"If I write things, I get them perfectly clear,
but if I talk, it always sounds the most
frightful muddle; and that's why I never
discuss my plots with anyone."

—Ariadne Oliver, *Dead Man's Folly* (1956)

"That's the curious part about speaking
the truth. No one does believe it."

—Tuppence Beresford, *The Secret Adversary* (1922)

It is an odd feeling to have a book growing inside you, for perhaps six or seven years knowing that one day you will write it, knowing that it is building up, all the time, to what it already *is*. Yes, it is there already—it just has to come more clearly out of the mist.

—Agatha Christie, *An Autobiography* (1975)

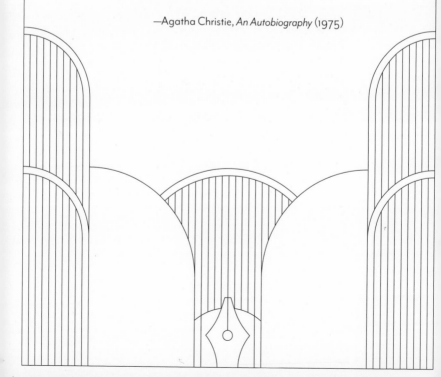

If you like to write for yourself only . . . you can make it any length, and write it in any way you wish; but then you will probably have to be content with the pleasure alone of having written it.

—Agatha Christie, *An Autobiography* (1975)

Certainly, when you begin to write, you are usually in the throes of admiration for some writer, and, whether you will or no, you cannot help copying their style. Often it is not a style that suits you, and so you write badly.

—Agatha Christie, *An Autobiography* (1975)

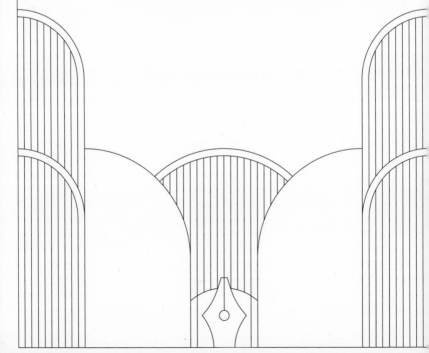

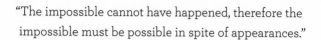

"The impossible cannot have happened, therefore the impossible must be possible in spite of appearances."

—Poirot, *Murder on the Orient Express* (1934)

It may be stupid, badly written, no good at all. But it was written with integrity, with sincerity, it was written as I meant to write it, and that is the proudest joy an author can have.

—Agatha Christie, *An Autobiography* (1975)

Some of my books satisfied and pleased me. They never pleased me entirely, of course, because I don't suppose that is what one ever achieves. Nothing turns out quite in the way you thought it would when you are sketching out notes for the first chapter, or walking about muttering to yourself and seeing a story unroll.

—Agatha Christie, *An Autobiography* (1975)

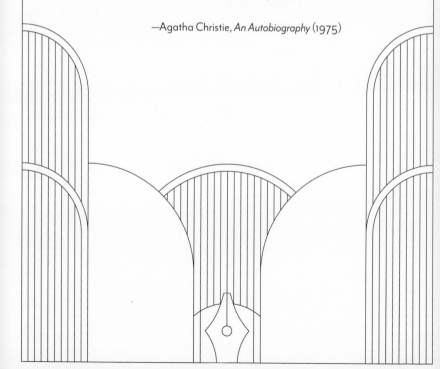

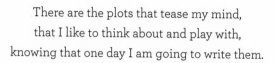

There are the plots that tease my mind,
that I like to think about and play with,
knowing that one day I am going to write them.

—Agatha Christie, *An Autobiography* (1975)

I suddenly found that the book was
becoming rather fun to write.

—Agatha Christie, *An Autobiography* (1975)

ISBN 978-1-7972-2627-9

Manufactured in China.

MIX
Paper | Supporting
responsible forestry
FSC™ C136333

Design by Wynne Au-Yeung.

10 9 8 7 6 5 4 3 2 1

See the full range of Agatha Christie gift products at
www.chroniclebooks.com.

Chronicle Books publishes distinctive books and gifts. From award-
winning children's titles, bestselling cookbooks, and eclectic pop
culture to acclaimed works of art and design, stationery, and journals,
we craft publishing that's instantly recognizable for its spirit and
creativity. Enjoy our publishing and become part of our community
at www.chroniclebooks.com.

Special quantity discounts are available to corporations and
other organizations. Contact our premiums department at
corporatesales@chroniclebooks.com or at 1-800-759-0190.

Chronicle Books LLC
680 Second Street
San Francisco, California 94107
www.chroniclebooks.com